phloem

phloem

Old Poems
1983 - 2022

Marguerite Bunce

PUNCHER & WATTMANN

First published in 2025
Published by Puncher and Wattmann
PO Box 279
Waratah NSW 2298

https://www.puncherandwattmann.com
web@puncherandwattmann.com

ISBN   978-1-923099-59-3

Cover image by Michael Slusakowicz
Cover design by David Musgrave
Typesetting by Morgan Arnett
Printed by Lightning Source International

NATIONAL
LIBRARY
OF AUSTRALIA

A catalogue record for this work is available from the National Library of Australia

for my father,
John P. Bunce

Contents

Clearly, that – is a tree –

Clearly, that – is a tree –
but your name has made it whole and small, and
I cannot fit those thirty half-sour
oranges upon me anywhere, nor can I
include this half-bitten leaf with
the viridian curve of shade and spines.

One of those spines has caught
me near my eye while I squeeze my
nose against the bees for a smell
of orange blossom from such precise
flowers that the whole of this seizure
is caught by them – and their
seasoning is such that the sting above
my eye and the history of bees which
is my own private association – and the
sun and mock orange for brides
on Spanish rooves all seem
to be caught in my sense of our tree.

But not just this tree, where your finger
points; I have had others, two
in my possession. An old seville
half-wild with thorns from its root
stock, in a bed set with sandstones.
Its shape was like the old-days, like
my big dulled pennies and its blossom
dizzied bees from streets away. The oranges
were small and hard, but the oil from their rind

lathered my hand when I squeezed fifty
for a pint of vigorous, bitter syrup.
The other was my junior. It fed on manure
from cows with names, and grew oats higher
than its trunk from undigested, unhusked grain.
Navel and green, that fruit was watched;
watered with soapy cast-offs until orange
and bird pecked, I bagged twenty for my city
flat. One at a time they were the essence
of all oranges, the template and paragon for all
that followed.

Now I can say – tree – if you like,
but understand the conditions.

Summer Storm

And you remember when the afternoon
        was a bowl
    bound and bevelled by home

washing and washing with air
        through large-holed wire
    and you cry to remember summer.

No-where was there
        ever a storm
    strewing beyond the mesh of your window

like the one which repeated
        all one year –
    when some hay bales reminded you

lose, you lose, you lose more
        mostly when
    that saucer you live in has no rim.

Orchard

This swatch of land
    fibrous to its boundaries
    is ordered with fruit trees
    whose twigs are mad.

The cutting is awkward
    so tedious he prunes
    long before the pink bark glows
    for better fruit.

By spreading branches
    stripping grey filigree
    till clean and open
    low for reach;

so they come good
    for the seasonal crates
    matching the labels
    with profusion and sap.

And women always write of love.

Flowering Time

It is bitter to be resident of a house built on sand; like the churlish
   flannel flowers
I have returned to Hilltop, in the heat.
There is nothing clean in this expanse of land, neither in my eyes, nor
   in your colours.

We are all clouded with a residue of salt, seasoned while unripe, it
   overpowers,
and our sour youth has set – complete.
It is bitter to be resident of a house built on sand, like the churlish
   flannel flowers.

You are dislodged like the rest, by a fire, autumn, rain or some
   abandoned car
but you can stay in this curry-smelling bush; it hurts that, unlike me
   you are returned to your seat.
There is nothing clean in this expanse of land, neither in my eyes, nor
   in your colours.

Only my leaving is permanent, though I can see my trees pale – through
   the heat, I have joined the travellers
who visit to draw, to press, till even these flowers are made to seem
   sweet.
It is bitter to be resident of a house built on sand, like the churlish
   flannel flowers.

But some years, you tell me, are not for show at all; you withdraw
and cower,
and if you resemble me, it is an act of denial, not retreat.
There is nothing clean in this expanse of land, neither in my eyes, nor
in your colours.

I dislike you for what you show of me, the small tight meanness, the
slow persistent loss of powers.
Once I lived here all the time, angry, lonely; never have I left this
place alone, in peace.
It is bitter to be resident of a place built on sand, like the churlish
flannel flowers.
There is nothing clean in this expanse of land, neither in my eyes, nor
in your colours.

Subdivision – a tale of four houses

My memory is clear on one point.
    Poplar leaves have hidden the perspective
    lines, and waiving farewell, the non-distance
    shines with their impressionistic glints.

    It is unfathomable to be so small in your own dream:
    flattened with respect for my backdrop, and yet
    I am small at the time
    when I lived in a childhood home, full
    of instances;

can I add that when I was three I fell
    hands first into a fire, and covered in cotton wool
    emerged from the doctor's, red with embarrassment.
    Full of details, too, this home was to become many,
    like an old orange splitting on the bush. Into four
    where once the front the back the side had been;
    and I became a counting-bead with all my trees notched up
    beside me. Goodbye, I soured, and came to move south.

    Allied with young trees, I built a foreground
    from sight, screening in stages, my extensions.
    The new house had front and back, the sides thin
    participants in the passage of rows of perennials hanging
    the perimeter with semi-substance.
    Under layers of pre-maturity
    I grew. One house became two.

I looked over my fence, and left.
    At last I could give trees no number, often
    no name. An abyss of foliage and rooms; at night
    it was night – relief
    from counting in the day. The absent abacus
    left me time: I filled with running things.
    They fed and ran and were carried away.
    Not sure of my bounds: where one scrubby stick
    became someone else's, I, too, spilled over.
    I seethed inside my house, expanding with the wood-steam.
    Soon enough,
    these days were measured
    in the small of my kitchen; while someone else's sticks
    turn in the stove, my dream becomes this place
    of two years, a bubble from my head.

I have grown an engrossing eye now,
    living in a balloon of clothes and books.

The Things He's Seen

Of course, they've all got war stories,
that summer in Darwin with a trainload
of rotten cabbages; but he's got visions
of impossible time, time cut out like movie frames.

Reginald Thorald, a mate of Dad's, spends time
as it turns out, recovering from himself.
The War missed his arm, a fence at Walcha found it.
The first stage of a war, first scene, the action
slowed down. 'I was just getting through the fence, I'd
put the gun over then damn me if I couldn't see
that bit of smoke, before the bullet, right
down into the barrel. And if I can see it,
it must be going to get my eye.'
But it went clean through the inside
elbow, that nice clump of veins with the trustworthy
hinge. Reg took shape: the exotic
one-armed farmer and erstwhile Insurance man.

And they're funny, boiling with laughter grabbing
his shoulder, Reg ends one and begins another. The story
of the cow and calf, himself between them,
on a horse, as they thunder together
into a truculent, cow-like reunion. 'Of course
the horse bucks, and I'm looking down onto the tree tops.
I must be fifteen feet in the air. Next thing
I'm looking right up the nostril of this
bloody cow, and I think: one of us is on
his back.' It's him, and he's amazed at the way
his brain has worked.

The last time we saw him
his index finger had just been sewn back on;
one of his calves and a nylon rope
had collaborated after feeding to become
a scimitar. With an almighty tug and no pain, Reg
had a piece of rough skin and his picture
of a four-fingered future to look into.

Margaret Preston's Vases Speak

Not quite at the centre,
but focal thing, nonetheless.
A great white lump
with all my insipid friends
sitting in what looks like thin
scrambled egg
with fruit.
Summer.
She thought 'white light –
breakfast –
serviceable china'
And for flowers
all the imported lightweights
have been trotted out
like cross-stitch samplers.
Too simple, too calm.
(I need a domestic
upset)

Summer 1915

Who would have expected
the Native Pea
to be pretty.
She obviously hasn't grown
up in the homely world
of the Eggs and Bacon bush.
The rotten wiry plant
with the hard nut
flowers, and stems that didn't
snap but twisted into rope and tore.
The flowers loved from desperation
and the lack of anything else
to play with.
And they're all jammed
together – a European cluster
the bush couldn't begin to fathom –
in an ugly glazed bucket
stupid with joy.

Native Pea – Australian Wildflowers 1923

Yes   yes
Yes   yes I know
what you're thinking – crimson –
tight-lipped, trite, tea-party colour,
but I,
chief tea-pot, know
better – look what she's done
with it, it's enough
to make you want to throw
cakes
at the hostess, grab fistfuls
and eat the icing
squeezed onto the knuckles.
Only a violent
red-headed woman
paints a pink checked tablecloth
with a blood-red
lacquer tray
and lets them bulge.
Where is the afternoon
of the occasion? Our cross-eyed
handles give off
no view; we have shouldered
the burden of decorum
while she
roughs up
a fully finished piece
of work.

Thea Proctor's Tea Party 1924

Ultra marine.

Svengali has nothing
on this blue; this is the blue
that will require no action
impose no desire – look into
this water and you can reflect
on nothing.
I am a blade of grass
on its edge – a stroke
scraped in a surface – a negative –
a thing – mesmerised.

It is not possible
to focus on the lighthouse – it could not
be weaker – the warning would come
too late, the immersion already complete.
Eyes weak at the knees – compelled
into that slow blue, those trees
of spike, those sails like teeth,
I'm almost at sea
with this unfathomable
prospect.

Sydney Heads 1925

Ah, Jocasta.

I have given myself
a name
which sounds like emerald
green with thick black
lines and a touch
of magenta; a wide base
and full body
no neck, but a twisted
handle.

Jocasta and Protea –
the partnership of two
minor gods – in the perfectly
tragic proportions
of heavy-handed
bliss. A mourning card
happily received; we are
a black-edged, thick-headed
delight.

We kill peasants'
children and show old people
gold.
We watch a princess
put three silk dresses
into a walnut shell.
We drug ourselves
with each other
to stay upright.

Protea 1925

I have been misrepesented.
The artist is my enemy.
My counsellor, the thorny leaf
on the extreme right
has said – in words to this
effect: 'Get out of bad
relationships – you
are a victim of the artist's
circumstance – her naïve
discolourations have coarsened you –
she is no Plato – her template
for you is no more
than a hybrid willow-pattern –
sell your soul – and this
is what you'll get.'
I look into my glaze
and see – that I am a prop
for these anemones. Red houses,
fish-bone fern, vandyke teeth
upon my handle, a mess
of orange.
The outrage of orange!

I am a Greek hydra
at the bottom of the sea –
and the anemones –
for reflected glory –
attach themselves
to me.

Anemones 1925

I don't know how
she found me – there were no
junk shops then – they were
only just producing these things.
There weren't art pottery shops
like you have now, love.
Maybe one of her friends
made me; but there weren't many
so strongly influenced by
Modern Art to produce a
cylinder and expect
a nod and a smile. I mean
look at me, a sawn-off
set of binoculars,
sticking up.
She only used me for banksias,
bless their little spines.
'You glorious ocular
balance' – she'd say, pushing
her nose at me while she plunged
the stems in. 'Gaud' – I'd think –
'what a nutter'.

Banksia 1927

Ellipses and lines
sit still in the life
of a modern
kitchen table;
crammed halves
and chromatic weight rest
on two legs;
browned-off black
and white turn the 20's
grey and cream.
Does Margaret
really have
such a corner
in her kitchen?
In undiluted order
do we find
a stew?
Are the apples
on the scale
meant for the pot?
Kitchen bliss –
has anything ever been
so chaotically
clean?
Have shadows
ever been
so fine?
What
can you make
of it.

Still Life 1927

There you are
you thirties thing, uh
no, twenties
art deco; or cold hard
gorgeous steel from the age
of machine-love
when machines with puppy fat
had idiosyncratic virtues
of design: you thing –
six, counting shadows
set for chess or just
casting round.
Cups are pawns –
the jug's bishop, castellated sugar cup –
rook, glass of water (with half lemon, immersed)
– an incongruity, can't fit.
See: there's that element
of silliness to the cold hard
facetious fact.
Implement Blue
how do you do?

Implement Blue 1927

God, how I love those flowers –
for I am their dish of water
and their retainer.
When one, through heaviness
of soul – overbalances – and its stem
like Tantalus, is stiffened
in air – I hate my shallow
rim and grieve
long hours for its succourless
proximity and memorise the details
of every turgid cell before the colour
runs.

I have been gum blossom
for two days – let me show you
the veins of the leaves,
they are red, all the shades
of chlorophyll making dashed
strokes through rhomboid blocks
of matured green.
When placed in me,
anointed as it were, flowers, stems and leaves
attain a kindly ecstasy –
an apotheosis
of our hearth life.

Australian Gum Blossom 1928

Cipher. Waddaya godda
sigh for yourself:
>   just like the bottom
>   half of a soda syphon
>   with three planed glass
>   sides:
>   a vessel
>   which lets you see
>   the stalks and water level – but
>   brush strokes slur
>   the meniscus rim.
>   Then those white panels
>   at the rear – they
>   screen their meeting edges,
>   obscure their purpose;
>   they are strange
>   unfinished walls, flaking off
>   the black back drop.
>
>   A logical choice
>   from her collection
>   of vayses, a pleasing
>   equivalence between
>   the width of the leaves
>   and my see-through
>   glass facets.
>
>   Maybe you have noticed?
>   My scalloped top edge
>   mirrors (you joke)
>   the three taut caps
>   of Western
>   Gum Blossom.

Show and tell (hide and seek):
my (clear-cut) role
as support for the arrangement;
we join hands
(in a croquembouche of style)
for a partnership
of give (and take).

Western Australian Gum Blossom 1928

Crazy path pot
and lid.
Pre-patio, pre-sandstone
veneer; glossy.
Forget the flowers
they're dead.
I'm it.
Me and the
back-drop,
we're as palatable
as dirt, or
cave paintings –
pumpkin,
but authentic,
nice. We're
what you
get used to about
being Australian.

The Brown Pot 1940

Next to some other
things, on top of the book-case
next to a lamp stand and long necked
head, under some original
paintings, I lived at Berowra.

Not much attention
was paid me;
outside with the banksias
was the place
to be.

We lived
a very still life, almost purely
ornamental. Bereft
of begonias, we of the dust haze
sat unfilled.

I lived, an anachronistic
delicacy, inside a house
set in the bush,
at Berowra.

I lived at Berowra 1941

Noah with all his
dingbats –
cute Christianity
ain't for me –
I like my stories
straight – like a glass
of scotch;
I don't fit –
in fact,
I'd be insulted if
she'd asked:
'Please consider ...
turn to the right ... just
a little ... oh yes
just stay
like that ...'
But she didn't –
she's turned her cheek
and won't even look
sideways.
I've been left
on the shelf –
miles
from
the decanter.

Noah's Ark 1950

The vase of black glaze
aches.
The vase broaches
a complaint
to the artist
in the full sorrow
of a vassal:

'I do not want
such flowers – such as these
should be set
ten feet apart
upon their own
thick
umber stems
with the grey and green smoke
screen of the bush
to put them
in their place.
Their gathered
strength is like
flexing muscles
and my neck
feels their expansion
but keenly.'

Fool vase, in reply
you have been granted
the glassy eyes
of reflection.

Banksia 1952

There are no vases
inside a
bark lean-to.

The dark ages
began when she turned
aboriginal.

No more tea
parties; the flowers
stayed put

and got painted
how they grew,
willy nilly

or wild
in abstracts,
with no stems.

But the patterned guts
of kangaroos
were preferred

in crude clay
colours. I don't
overly care

for the primitive
origins
of porcelain.

POP

The old man moved into his night,
while I called out of the day,
bright in his room; a room
once mine, where I had slept
in terror of bible figures
and a pattern of tight-bound
colours wound into a coil.

I came to his room, a fly
to heat and light; remembering him
a summer thing of mustard cigar beer
ham olives – smells of men
swelling into laughter the size of waves.
Leaving my night to itself,
I caught him moving into his.

Her Mother's Voice

I

It is now that I want to roll with unlikely animals,
squirm cow dung through my fingers; squat over cabbage seedlings
feel their tedious growth with my nose, avenge them
of their enemies. That between-light with the smoke dim on the hills
and the cows arrogant in the paddock tinted pink, urges me
to run fast, skid and fall.

II

I am having a difficult childhood, catching odd moments
of idiocy and correcting them with the rod my father planted
in my head. Indecent frivolity
must be lapsed into, or earned vicariously
like the friendship of a two mile bush walk which ends
in rainbow cake illness with my mother. Recreation
is good for you – yes, and I must fight to relax too.
I must hide the copied drawings of birds I make, because
I am no artist.

III

My latest child is an independent chicken, born
two days ago to a fancy breed mother:
an idiot chook sitting heavy on dead eggs while calling,
conscientiously to her shrinking yellow blob on legs. An odd sight,
this unnatural mother with her adopted scrawn,
protecting itself already from a delicately offered

meal of whole corn, by picking bran off
the lumpish beak.
I compare our childhoods and feel cheated.

IV

Fifty years ago I watched cows wallow
towards the Island, towed behind a boat to a house
roaring with cousins and aunts. Dissolving our joints in water,
we sometimes heard tinkering noises from miles across;
while sheltering under Grandfather's figs, or rolling
on barrels of molasses, we were ferried across the swelling depression,
like most precious beasts.

V

Now I am five. Waiting in the mountains for the fruit
my Grandfather brings on weekends, I sit goading ant lions
in the early, heat-stricken morning. I live in the mountains
because we have moved to my Grandfather's cottage
at Springwood. I have scaled the silence of this place
after a long and confused starvation. Now I play solitary games
and walk; a serious brown child, with thick legs. I rush
for the fruit my Grandfather brings. Brittle in heatwaves,
my friend and I stuff bottles with food, rock them to sleep,
then smash them in their wicked, rancid maturity.

VI

When Soapie Hudson went off to join the war,
he left his house full of dogs and enough food
to last the day. After a while, they let the dogs go.

Once, when he had driven from his ridge to ours,
he let me drive his dray. In a vague, kind way
the slow turn of night becomes his return –
thickening my vigilance, he enters my fear.
I listen: they say there is a madman on the other side,
an artist with nude women all through his garden.
What do I think – it is growing, my picture.
There is richness in my twig life, coating my thoughts
with the moss velvet of folds and linings.

VII

My father is a signature in the first volume
of reference books which are mine. An empty
tin of 'Town Talk' tobacco is what I find
to imagine him in New Guinea, mustering Japanese.
With his brothers, he has built a rough, waist high
stone wall, at the front of my house.
It is not his face in this photo, though
I have always felt warm, being held by a man
smiling and dissembling as my father. Thumbed loose,
like green peas in a metal pot,
I am rolling on my stubbed stem of disbelief.
With his detachment, he is kind in his support
for others; but for me
he rattles and falls in faceless disappointment.

VIII

I am alone with my mother, while she smokes
waiting for bright lights, for men to go dancing
with. Half-deaf in the ringing bush, she hears nothing

and wants her gay life to start. Needing no
mirror, she sees herself blooming, encumbered with dullness.
Her skin, her eyes and legs compete with mine.
I am no competition, it is a pity. I am only a foil
absorbing and reflecting her obscene lust for better company.
She brushes my hair, stroke by stroke, courting
my cringing back, squeezing out my distress.
I strike hard; flouting my need for beauty, my foundling eye,
she grinds her thick lips into my face and demands
a sisterly confidence. I am seven,
and she will never hear my answer.

IX

Nor will you. Gentle as you are, you take my meandering
steps and set them in plaster, and will show them, eventually,
to anyone. How can I let the intimacy of my faltering
get out – when even my name on paper,
an old envelope or prescription bottle, is too specific
for garbage, or too precious.
And what am I protecting: have I, mistakenly,
put my life into a capsule
that only I can swallow; or is it that each day
many unconnected things must remain
dark and humid, just in case.
So I will not tell you any more; you will do
what you like with what you know already
from twenty odd years of traces, and of course,
you have your own collection of my days.

X

Each barely broken morning she lies in bed
tracking cows and distant, secretive vehicles
as they cross her broad window. The distance
of the view is both new and a return to when,
enveloped in a bush gulley she dissolved into young eyes.
Too late, because she dare not try to run, or crush
calves with her hands, or even catch the boundaries
of this land with her heel. Only her eyes
can move with the relief of this return.
In the half-light she sees
each day of her childhood has grown
into a solitude of chooks and aeroplanes and persistent weeds –
but her adult life is as taut and confused as the yawning
howl of a bush dog at night, asking or claiming
his right to this place.

Someone Jumped From Australia Square

(from a family of cashmere and chocolate –
in the centre of racing circles, the auctioneers
of yearling pure-breeds, whose youth
danced in sprung jarrah ballrooms, and whose middle-age
leased offices in the city)

When you cut me out,
there were gaps and holes – you mixed me up
with the horse and the jockey – I was shot
with limbs, and slubbed with their mud.
When you cut me out, it was fine wool
you chose, a binding as close as thirty years
of anything.

I flap loose a fold of my suit as I walk
in slow rolling strides:
we all gather at the crossing, I would
rip silk, if I could.

I spill coffee every morning, it soaks
into the crumbs on my tie. It is here that I sit
in my tightening suit, twenty-seven floors up –
a freeze framed Icarus on butter-cake clouds.

This suit, you see, is my weighting.
I can only fly so high, and that, with help. My wings
are fixed, my fall – controlled.
The sweat and urge of the turf do not need
me, I simply divert their heft

into pattern. Because I am – this
heavy thing.

    If I were a rose bush,
    if I were a bush of roses, if I breathed
    rose, slept rose – died with every rose
    a full – arm, hand, fist – blown
    life, a red wealth in a bed
    of many, I would fall like horses feet.

My office friends and I are going
to the Club; we are falling, feet first,
together, and landing, stiff. My fellow
stripes and I are having lunch
on the second floor, under a heated
swimming pool: there is no water stain, no sign
of diving-damp – I crack my joke. My fellow
blotting pads and I are eating beside
portraits of punters and horses. We are getting up
and releasing our creases, we are walking
back down Elizabeth Street, we are entering
our upward draft.

    I cannot see the whole of myself
    in any mirror that I know. My maker
    is therefore, incomplete; a fashioner
    of compromised shapes, a cripple who will
    not risk the mount of Pegasus.

But she was trying, aiming for my mouth,
to make me talk; she was edging round my lips
and wringing her sticky words at my ear.
She thought, that I, in my afternoon drone
would carry her hollow baggage, and find
her home. Then she finally heard the smallness
of her name in my voice and hung-up. So I presume
she is on the flight to Ely Cathedral: and the sky
is matte blue, and the stars are asterisks, and her wings
are immobile and certain – as she hovers through
her magic tableau of resilience.

I see squares and letters from a circuit
tower, and I am not so high at all, to be still
in a maze of slurred order, to be
sinking in a stiff dirge. For
I have looked from this window
at the wrong time –
I have formed the will to skin my life –
scrape clean this sponge of gridded wool.

In this act of my own paring, I am liquid
and resolved. Inside me
is a rose, releasing my colour
falling soft and apart. Inside me
is a violent rose, a rose
in a must of thorns. I have hammered them out
and stuck them fast – they are the shivering
scales of my wings, they are the shrieking sound
of my flight.

And so mother, father and maker
I have flown and landed,
I have found my fullness
in a pool of splintered red –
still steaming in the sun's fractured heat.

A Mechanical Life

My Car by Marguerite Bunce

My car is yellow. It has the smallest wheels
of any on the road: Pirelli steel
radials, because I love it so.

The Stanley lights are big and round: at night
my beam has the crossed eyes of a delicate child; we go
on long trips, like foolish virgins in the dark.

Under the bonnet, its engine goes chirr. People say it sounds
like a bike going past – but so what. 'Well,
your bike sounds like a can-opener', I yell out fast.

The roof is dented. Some jerk sat on it one afternoon,
like a cardboard cushion; and the creases left
by that drunk goon creak and wallop as I polish it.

At each service station, the attendant learns
about the metal flap with a secret spring
inside the door, to protect and hide my petrol cap.

It costs $8 to fill 'er up. A full tank
gets to Mittagong and back, with a bit left over for the city,
but I usually ask for 'five bucks worth, thanks'.

ITS EXHAUST

There it is, that one, no, the one
behind. The yellow one, daffodil
yellow, and there,
under the bumper bar, just
come round a bit, see its
stainless steel bum-gut.
My shiny
protruding pipe has a
ten year guarantee, and my big idea
is to replace
the rest of its mortal
parts and build a car,
a perfect city car, a second-hand
master car, a Phoebus'
cart – a car of stolen
thunder,
making the god of new
cars wince.
I know this is hubris.
That over my fortunate wheel
loom portents
of
rear-visionary
destruction.

DEUS EX MACHINA

It's ten to eight when we get
into the car, on a Friday night in reflex city
and head for Broadway, turning
right then
left into Cleveland Street.
And if at first I give
instructions like this, it's
to stake a claim to my stretch
of moving – I'm going somewhere. But
earnest trundling annoys the Friday night
cars; the big city music gets louder, these FAST CARS
BITE, they've got to
get away, accelerate
flex
and swerve to escape the diminutive
effect of this car next to theirs, getting somewhere.
The big city lights go flash-flash
on the big tar flash
floor, and to them
my car must be
some faithful horror, some monogamous
frump. They're artery cars main-lining
movement: ol' capillary
an' me jus' cloggin' things
up. At the lights, stopped, waiting to
turn into George
Street, Redfern, I say to the scoffing
person at my side – 'I love
this car' – this car which courses
with the adrenalin of the

follow, swallows with a not meek
air, the exhaust of carbon-copies
re-aligning. *O city machine,*
you fill me
with trembling.
I say 'I love this
car', I turn to his face with a finger
flick laugh and my head goes
dashboard, neck-brace, dashboard,
I'm having an accident.
Oh no.

OUT OF THE CAR

Men were made
for accidents. At accidents
you see them out
of the car and running
towards you and away
from you
doing everything right
around you in orbit, like
they're driven, pulling
faces, together, rubbing at
the damage, writing out
details, taking turns to use
the phone, greasing the cogs
of your
accident.
He's out there. There's
the blur of his coat
in speed fins
behind him, but around
me, still
idling, about to
jerk off
the blinker, off the engine, get
out, but O binomial me, he's gone
round three times at least and
now he's back
with a card
in his hand, O
where's the other car,
he says it's here,

I've got its number
from a taxi driver.

I don't believe
it's gone I saw no lights
I heard no swerve, this
calling card,
don't give it to me, I'm
out.

SUSTAINED DAMAGE

What can I do but smile, with a big soppy female
face while I watch the footpath heroics of my little
black bakelite thug, going hell for leather under the bonnet; backed
up against the manifold and head-locked
by the grill, my petrol pump keeps punching
out its guts through a ruptured fuel line.

The Law of the Land

It's my first
time with a policeman.
I'm all quivering
ready to be delivered
and refined in
the process of the law
mowing down my
enemies, sifting good
from weevil.
In the young girl
clothes, pinks
and russet browns,
my scare-crow
brain is making
threshing
waves; O
the police, the police, they
gather you up in
the full sweep
of their strong arm
which will
outstretch
flex and sever on my
behalf.
And with
a flail of eye to eye and
hand (I do
I will)
I gust the shred
of evidence

to the constable-in-charge
of fresh faces. He says,
ring us Monday,
and it drops
away, the heavy-headed burden of
just so much accurate
and spirit-level
a last straw left
to flummox
and dandle
with the
husk of my
car.

undercarriage

My mother never told me to wear
clean presentable
underpants in case I was laid
prone
by an accident. She was too
surprised I had worn
none at Bankstown
Airport when I was five
to bother.

But it's exposure,
that's what an accident
is. There,
in the dark,
in your car, protected
by the road rules
and medical cover, insurance cover – bang –
you're an accident. And each time
your name, address, car
registration is divulged, another layer
comes off.

And to the people driving past,
on-lookers, policemen
and tow-truck
drivers, you have been singled
out by the phony
intimacy of a public
redressing
its victims.

But she's out there, on the street, with her
leaf suspension – left rear
quarter panel and stone
guard all hitched-up, bumper bar
cocked, buckled boot, crimped trim, pleated
numberplate – fistfuls of creased
metal skirting, standing in
a coy Monroe pose.

CARNAGE

Just think
of all the flesh
a hospital gets
rid of –
contents of themselves that
people had had ideas
about. They
only had an involuntary
ownership and when
it came
to the crunch
a wilful vagueness
about functions and positions and
only a nominal command
over their vented spleen and
breaking heart.

FIRST BLOOD

At the time
our bodies started
giving way, our class was taken
to the See-through Woman.

Her plastic reproductive lumps and tubes
were as much a Cyberman's as mine; the freak
show names and feminine functions
predicted Visceral Horror would occur within
our life-times.

It was sometime
in adolescence I
turned to bits and pieces
and from then on – anything –
could go wrong.

And the accident, my machine's
menarche revealed
the raw details of my
car's mutable
parts.

_ _ _ _ a poke

I understand Eddie
Azzopardi now.

Some wisdoms
start
as an itch. Thin
layers of frustration
growing round a grain of something
wrong, and the stretched skin around a milky
lustred product,
scraped from a clamped
shell,
has no value
for those before whom
it is spread.

By Monday my
constable
had baulked. His in-tray was slopping across
his desk. There
were so many accidents
like mine, I had to give
him time, he'd tell me what I
needed to know, things were getting out
of his hand, like who
gave out the address of the car's registered
owner, and who
told me, the morning after
the accident, that the car –
a late model green Jaguar –

had been picked up? Because
there was nothing. There was nothing like that.
In fact it was likely that there
never would be anything.
I should let
him
get on with things, and get off
his back.

Constable,
why?

Constable,
why was I
rogered?

Constable,
why was 'Pig fingers
Bacon' – written on the wall
of the Glebe Coroners'
Court?

Constable, why,
when you were so weighed down with the work
of justice and truth,
why
did I think
that you
might join
others
and fly?

CARCASE (A Maori called Wayne)

My friend and I took them on. In an HR holden
wagon we drove to an address out west. Of course, we weren't meant
to have this address, and the local police
had been there before us. They'd knocked at the door, stood there
with the dog barking, seen the caravan in the driveway, just as we
had. And been told, by a woman in her fifties, that the person
they were looking for, didn't live there anymore.
We heard the dog, and waited. We'd started to look around the back
when the caravan door opened and an old bloke stepped out. No,
she hasn't lived here for ages. And hearing that, the police
must've left. Couldn't they smell it?
Blood.
The stuff which is thicker than water.
Who did live there?
Mum.
Who were we after?
Her estranged daughter Jan.

We rang Mum
a lot.
Family relations improved
rapidly.

I'm not the car's owner any more, Jan said. And don't bother
my mother.

We smelt something else, then. Something light
as air. Channelled into pipes running just under
the ordinary, the everyday, the smell you don't want to leave
behind, but you do. Our Jan talked nice, but she'd just let

off.

I'll get in contact with the real owner and he'll contact you.

After a while
we rang Mum.

Jan rang us. There was to be
a Barrister. Everything's going
through him, she said. He'll contact you.

We found his number and got him first.
No,
he didn't want any more contact with these people, and had
put them onto
a Solicitor.
This
Solicitor, wasn't in the phone book, he wasn't listed with the Law
Society. His contact number was an establishment
so licensed
it was hard to make the contact. Or the date.
We got our own
Solicitor. He
set up the date.

Their man was
late.
He needed to sit down. His eye
was blood-shot, and his pin
striped legs
were wobbly. His client,
on the other hand
was 'hot-headed' and

'toey'.

Negotiations jammed. We had to ring Mum,
late.
And I got rung
late, too.
We were all playing
dirty. And suddenly someone got the wind
up.
The police rang.
We were given an address and a name;
we were told not to try and contact *him*.
                    ?
On a short drive, the address was found to be
non-existent. My constable said, sorry, he'd
mis-read it. Try this one.
And by the way, he's come
into the station. Apparently, he lent
his car to one of his regular
drinking
mates, a Maori
called Wayne, who borrowed it on Friday
and brought it back Monday with smashed
in head lights.
He hasn't been heard
of since, and no-one knows
his sur
name.

But our man's been
booked for withholding information.

A woman answered.
Was it Jan? At his door? It was hard
to catch him
in. Even though, on each of the three
occasions, someone was inside. But
finally we got
another date. Eight
am. His place. His manager.
Of
His Affairs.

We are offered coffee
while we wait
in the Jaguar's den. Our man is big
and nervous. Pacing while he drinks
more filtered coffee with a couple
of pills
thrown in.
Clive is running late. We make,
very small
talk. Things get tough when Clive
arrives.

'Your car is worth one cent.' He also said.
'My mate's on edge.'
His mate sank more pills and shook
his head.
So I said.
No matter what you think my car is worth. Some prick
ran into it. And some prick is gonna pay
what I think
it's worth.

We suggested 2,000. Clive laughed the bitter,
knowing laugh. While his mate was likely to do
anything, he was not.
The poor bloke had-no-money
the poor bloke shook his head
a sucker's sense of responsibility
(and a police record stored in a restricted file)
and was barred from driving for life
he just did them up to keep-himself-occupied
and if the truth
were known
he'd have to borrow from his adviser
Clive who was a used-car salesman – his mate,
and was an idiot – his mate added
to give us anything.

We left.
With $1,800.
Through the generosity
of the sucker's
heart.

In sides

The god of New Cars promises
everlasting life.

As the first article
of faith you take
out a comprehensive Insurance Policy.

His agents are everywhere. 'Are you insured?' the
police at the scene ask. 'Are you insured?' the tow-truck
driver asks, because if you're not
it's heresy
to be a victim
of fate.

The forces against
the unforseen
are legion. Feel encouraged
to gird your pockets, fill the plate; be prudent
and provident – they'll ensure
you believe
you'll get your money back.

Waiting on the threshold of another
church, where the Service
is continuous (8 to 4pm) and held by men
in over-alls, I enter
supplicant to the man
in charge. 'Is it
an Insurance job?' he asks.

My car

tucked neatly between my legs, leaves.
They won't even do
readings from the Manual without
a fifty buck deposit
refunded
when they get the job. Besides, there's
no room
in the workshop.

We move on
my write-off and I, all eyes averted from
the rust
stained left-rear quarter, searching for a
beater of panels, anything
but the purdah
of an unhallowed
wrecker's
yard.

Preservation Techniques

My car would not receive the
unguents
and lacquers from the high-priests
of the after-life, the panel
beaters.

Good as pre-loved
its innards were to be scooped
out of the old body
inserted
into another old body,
procured from someone's backyard. An
unorthodox practice, which the ministers
for Commodore and
Mercedes refused
to undertake, due to its straight for
ward procedure. (Resurrection takes
at least three days)

My body search
stopped on Mt Druitt. This western
suburb was the out-post
for carboys breaking in
Chargers and Mustangs,
and when they weren't re-mounting
their engines, they were lounging round
the car accessories bar in
Target. Here, father had bought son
a small car, for safety. Within a week, the car
had safely been driven to death.

I'd found father's ad in Trading
Post, hitched a trailer to the Wagon
and headed out towards
the land of five acre
wrecker's yards
with penned Impala and
Parisienne dinosaurs, rusting
alongside market
gardeners' haciendas
and villas sunk
in shimmering
paspalum plains. And there
I traded my yellow body
for red; sunrise
for sunset; jaundice
for venality.

THE *LATIN* SERVICE

All mechanics are disciples.
Their god has active suspension
technology
and other things
they are in awe of each time
they kneel, turn
and slide under
the latest model. What they see
when they look up
are their own limitations. No longer
capable of irreverent
improvisation – wafers of plastic-metal
sealed and blessed
by the dealer
are placed in absolute
position – for trans
ubstantiation must occur
before the supplicant can
rev
again
in a state
of grace called
showroom
condition.

A Mechanic named Paul

He was recommended as a man
who believed
in the value of old
cars. Actually making hot
rods by putting Civic
engines into Scamp
bodies and letting them
rip. So I left him with two cars
to get one
on the road.

It was called
a conversion. This process. But it was
interrupted by a strange occurrence.

Blinded by a halogenic
beam, wherein a voice said unto him:
'Why ignorest thou me?'
'Who are you?' he cried. 'I am your
Manufacturer, the supplier of all *new*
parts, and instigator of all *manuals*, I do this
to help you and all those who mistake
me for the *elder* Statesman,
my predecessor, who refused to hear the word:
Up-date.' And he, Paul, trembling and astonished said, Lord
what wilt thou have me do? And the Lord said unto him,
Arise, and wash the grease from your hands,
toil no more in the grime of ancient
engines, working for the enemy I have deemed:
Obsolete.' But Paul cried, 'What am I to do

with – this?' And the Lord replied 'Does it have fuel
injection?' Paul bowed his head. 'It is ordained of God
to be the Judge of quick and
dead. *It is* hard
for thee to kick against the pricks. So get your
assistant to finish it off, licketty split.'

Paul was unable to keep working on my
job, and gave it to his assistant,
who diddled the hours
on his time-sheet
and doubled my bill.

When I drove the car
away, it went at twenty miles an hour
and seized up after
half.

Those cars, Paul said,
don't go
much better than that. You should
have bought a
new car.

And it was then that I took the matter up
with the council of the Patriarchs, summarily
called, the Motor Vehicle Repairs Complaints Tribunal.

ALTERNATIVE HEALING

It was Wal
who fixed it up.
In his backyard at
Abbotsford, he bled
the brakes and stopped them
binding, changed the brake master
cylinder, connected the inhibitor
switch and loosened the automatic transmission
selector cable, connected all the wires again and altered
the toe-in, fitted the bonnet locking catch,
cable and anchorage, replaced the broken
CV boots and changed the back
left-hand shock
absorber
as well.

All this he did out of love
for Honda 600s, and my car, he said,
has a lovely engine
for its age.

Celebrity Knock Out

He starts his day
and so do I, 7am –
almost the same,
he and I, we
get up, get dressed, get in
our car, and I

am driving to Marrickville High,
from Glebe. To the Greeks and Lebs
who live a golden teenage
of puffed up chests
and smart arsed jokes. These kids

might know his name, the father of the son,
The Man, whose name's the same
and who's just started
playing
the beautiful game.

Why do we, we all know
their names, even if we
don't give
a toss for
the sport they played, play, get
sponsored for: the bash, thump, smash,
crash, king-hit, mash, concuss,
break, bust, crush, trounce
the opposition – action hungry boys all
watching the battl
ing big men, these

powerful stadia
filling men of roar
and cheering.

Taking a meander
of left, right, left and
then right, all the while
the traffic thrusts and lulls-
then straight, then stop, idle
then go. Liberty Street
takes me in its flow.

A white
4 wheel drive filled with boys
in white shorts, singlets
to be trained in the arts of stun
and bash, young contenders for the punch
ing ring. Swallow and swing
you choir boys, for the red satin
robes
and the big fat gloves of bene
diction – A
Man, the father of The, is a
bout to give
a lesson.

I've dropped
my guard. At the cross
street Cam
bridge has
the Cele
brity on the move and he's too

big to stop, too high
for low, too much mo
men
tum, all four white drive
wheels are
on their
way
through
my car.

For those of you
who think a brush with such
might be chance or luck: I got his name
and number on a little
piece of paper, and as he was
uninsured
and short of time, he
left the scene
of the crime. Like any old dick.

After which, my car was
parts.

Lazarus

I was there and where
I was was an old street of mine, a minx
of Mary with some dead end, in Glebe
in the dark. The dead of night. But lit
as all streets are, enough to see
that the car there was
in a state of abandon, collapsed – a can,
opened and emptied – a frame
for disgust or despair.

Without having ever searched, with loss
gone from my mind, the key was found
where I had never left it, in my hand.
The doors half open, were stiff hinged,
bashed, broken glass
filled the footwell, butt stubbed vinyl
and bags of rubbish – there it was,
in the rags of a beggar at the end of an odyssey,
revealed to Penelope, Martha rebuked,
all those myths of doubting women that I was not, not here,
not now, one of the ones who hope yet fear.
I knew.

So many years, and countries, and cars
had passed, but here I was again, with
my car, in the seat, turning the key. And
the engine – the sound which turned heads
when heard, 'there she goes', they knew
without looking the little car was passing –
turned over. The car of my dream
let me drive the one last time.

Où Sont Les Neiges

We are not unhappy here
for grey is the most subtle
and decorative of colours –
it folds us in a damp
and dirty flannel,
a thickness of our mother's
skirts – while we follow
the grid of her pins and
laces, and swallow the puffing air
of her grey powder. We traipse
and flounder – behind
her. We are two bears
on a string, if you like.

We have wandered
the warm places
and have sat with rich
lights and chipped cup sounds;
have seen delicate
windows of gauze.
And if they could be
felt, we would touch the black
curls of balconies, caught
undressing on the walls – or else
blow on the glass of their doors.

We have dropped like fools
into jam and swum
on rafts of caramel glaze

into walls of breaded pigs
and pamplemousse
preserves. Elegantly caught,
we watch our feet perfect
in amber, we window
the movements of our fingers
and toss our fur – thus.
We have been firm
as the smoke clears
to coals and the pot warms.
But our mouths crease
and hollow
through the toffee lacquer
as the taste
of vienna almonds settles
on our skin.
Our soft and slightly
mouldy guide has only just
unveiled the hags
with lemon-sucked faces
and house-maddened dogs.

And if you want to know
where we are now –
we have been left
in the white places
of blown grey and lifted
skirts. And in our heads, the grey
of every little thing builds
and caves open the starched flourish
of our eyes. The grey is only
something that we see. We are

clear and small, fallen as we
are, on the ground. We are not unhappy
here, only very few – and we have
failed to leave a trace.

Nothing
has ever been as awful
as the gravel outside the Louvre.

Occupied Territory

He has been gone a while, and though
I still watch the calendar and the hour
as they hum and drip their power,
my numbed blood grows deeper – like my face –
and darker, like my arms and I move
to the slow waltz of Spring in my hair.
With my nose and hands, I wear away
the skin of each day and crust dough
on my open mouth teasing these animal
threads of life, till they sing:
'Mr Mueller, I heard your horses screaming
and saw the black one die, his front legs
dragging the back, slowly, like a plough.'

Don't worry, it is nothing, it is war – inside is warm.

My love cannot love any more, not me
nor anyone else. He is tense –
like the axe in the abattoir.
Hovering over the trench
is his guardian angel who is
cutting the tops off roses and poppies
to relieve the boredom, the sullen
putrefaction of waiting.

Don't worry, it is nothing, it is war – inside is warm.

Two soldiers have come in the dark,
they want food, no – something to drink –

not water, when I offer it they laugh.
There is nothing else here, still they sit.
Then they laugh, then they laugh, pumping
it out, they laugh as they break, they laugh
as they break into me, pumping me full
of their time and their boredom till I
drag my sodden body away. Their laugh
leaks from me in gurgles, as I lie still.

Don't worry, it is nothing, it is war – inside is warm.

For what am I now, but a husk
for his grain, a pail seeping with his
milk; my waiting has become
his. For me, this war
has no blood; no blood has come
to relieve me of a life which will
slowly curdle and bubble till I choke it out,
and deliver it – his.
For what is left of me – the thin and silent brink
of gall and bile and acid – will wash
and caress his blind, growing flesh.

Don't worry, it is nothing, it is war – inside is warm.

And how you love the new green
of the trees. I see you in the wet morning
adoring the sun – hail fellow – you with
Apollo, giving and accepting, pumping
and laughing. The rise of the sun
for you, is everything, my rounding
has brought you this. Now you have place

you have footing; you have made yourself
at home. And how you love me.

　　　　　– it is nothing –

Our house grows fat with the soldier's
food – it is like a holy place, so rich
with the offerings my parents eat; while I,
the blessed idol, watch for the turning
to green, the slippery stench of the grease
the wondrous fullness of rancid incense.

　　　　　– inside is warm –

Yes, I am having your child, I am not
stone – for my stomach moves. Yes, feel it –
it is yours.

　　　　　– don't worry –

My time has come.
Is it for me – these drapes of gentle
care are folded and cleaned
and aired and scented – for me,
this glowering bloom of attendants,
this pain, this cursing, sucking
wrench, this child.
And what is it now, that you cry for –
your father is such a strong man, but
your mother is stronger still.
It is for me that we walk, you,
like wavering flannel in my loose

hands. Feel the wind
as I toss you
in the air, the ease
as I throw you off
this cliff.

Don't worry, it is nothing, it is war – inside is warm.

A Philanthropist's Pin-Up

There's a photo in the London Underground
of me – and I was pleased
ten years ago, when they took it

having no idea, as I do now
of the world between their ears
and up their noses, behind their eyes
and fattening their mouths
with what they couldn't say
to a seven year old blind girl:

listen potato-face, we want your picture
for a poster. You're just what we're
looking for. You're the blindest thing
we've seen.

And the bland girl's still there.

Don't give me that lost cherub's
face, those repulsively gentle
eyes, those contours like the mound
of growth covering a Roman wall;
this filled in balaclava is my head.

For them I'd now get my thumbs
in hard and press on my sockets.

Pubescence has given my
fingertips claws, I want red lips too. Make me

cheese-cake not rice pudding – I
want to hear lust from a mouth near mine.

That is unlikely,
I know. Console me,
let me feel – full –
so buy me shoes and I'd love
the lace holes; choose for me
a broderie anglaise dress; put me
in an art gallery and it's the stair-well
I'd love, for the gaps I fill
it must be seemly
so to do

oh yes, thank you, I'll
be a philanthropist's pin-up,
thank you.

Someone told me about the awnings
which appear, late spring, on buildings.
He described the feeling of a room
in which the sun is thwarted;
the dimmed heat on a hooded window. No-one
ever spoke before with such excitement
to me – I wonder what he looked like – I
wonder if he ever saw the black and grey
poster of a blind girl beside a stuffed lion –
her hand in its mouth: 'Visit the Natural
Museum – a unique experience for the blind.'

And by now we know,
what we should always have known, that
they are better at life
than we are. The creation
of family groups, caring
for the sick or suffering
beside them, the moving en
masse, to a better place, the in-built self-
defence even
the silent talking: they
do all this. And now
we know they did this all
along. We have no excuses:
pulp to paper
roll to wrap
toilet to hand
arse to wipe.
There is no redemption.
We will not be saved.
Might as well mumble
something sonorous:
"We therefore commit these bodies to the ground;
earth to earth,
ashes to ashes,
dust to dust"; now, let the histrionics begin:

DIE BACK

Quiet,

Quiet, please!

Right, then:

White Sally? Sorry. Snow gum? Black Sally?
Peppermint? Ummm. New England Peppermint?
Apple? Rough barked?

Ok.

take a deep breath – we rhyme with cheese

"Die back in Eucalyptus – its cause and cure" –
you've got to treat the thing a bit like a bikini:
briefly enough to be of interest, yet sufficient to cover the subject.

> Let's say that this is a talk on a subject,
> in conversational voices, about a problem
> which talks back. Are there any Ladies present? – Yes?
> I will begin again.

> I am going to tell the story
> of trees, of everything
> about trees – and you will not be able to see
> the wood – or the forest –
> for them.

front on, side on and multifarious: you can try

Shall I try to be Sibyl,
tell stories, stories
of facts so casually cryptic,
coptic, and coprolitic
that the message and the mystery,
the message in the mystery,
satisfy one and others'
desires?

copulate on me if you will, but only one at a time

Then I will live in the bole
of a tree; it will only be big enough
for me. Only through instinct
will I find it, through
simpleness – will you hear of it;
I will intumesce my words of wallow
forth: I will catalogue a mystery
and polish
a malignancy.

*First of all, we have to think of the eucalypt as not just a tree, but as
a habitat for other organisms, particularly insects and fungi.*

But I
have a picture of a tree:
der Baum, the tree of trees,
tree of no type or character –
a tree of balm.
Each leaf has been painted
exact in shades of verdant green
and laid, so they hardly
overlap, into a grand
circle of a crown.

Now this trunk, as this is the wrong
word, is in fact a stem
given the proportion but not
the bulk or vascular
bark of what it is to be – thickly –
trunk. It is what the mind
knows to be the link of tree
to ground: a concentration of leaves
into a long waist,
the middle of the hourglass
broadening, giving way
to the flaring that is never
seen but is rooted
in the mind as fibrous necessity.

Around this tree is air, the pure
blue air of dawn so virtuous
you can hear: "I have made
oxygen, it is my halo
in which I float." We all breathe –
it is empathy: "I rise like a hero,

watch my shadow swell; I protect,
I see; I am separate in all
my parts; I stand out."

But if you get past your interest in a plant, whether
it be a cabbage, or a dandelion, or a
tree, you find that the tree is just the first
step in the food chain. Other organisms eat it, others
use it as a house; galls on the underside of a leaf are
filled with eggs until the larvae are
ready to hatch.

wrestle with me

I have almost spoken with this German
tree but it has no character
and my eyes go wide – I think of
sunrise and Verdun –
European trees have more fun –
I thought that bottle blondes were plants –
natives, and that natives don't stand out,
they go backdrop; they dissolve; they hold your eyes
tight and filter light with grey and fill your nose
with mustard and in the bush you are alone
usually on a rock, and more alone because
you are there, scouring; scouring your thoughts
of the European shades of voluptuous
jealousies, outlines, silhouettes, cut-outs
until you ah native nut grass,
asking

And Nature, of course, always maintains a balance. In
undisturbed woodland for example, in northern New
England and the Western Slopes, you will find
you get a build up of predators which will defoliate
them. Then, perhaps, a bushfire comes along, wildfire,
unstoppable, and not only does it burn away the grass and cook
the trees and burn off the rest of the leaves but also
it kills the animal, the insect population, so, when the tree
sprouts anew, there are no insects to feed on the leaves and, for a few
years, once it has recovered from the fire, it is relatively free
from any kind of insect attack.

The Tree

Spring has brought
new life
to the Anthony Hordern tree
on Razorback Mountain
near Picton. The famous
landmark,
a 112 year old
Port Jackson fig, was given up
for dead
after being split
by a gale 3 years ago.
It resembles the oak
with which
the old firm
symbolized
its motto
"While I live I'll grow"

We have now, a picture;
we are driving past, over
the Razorback and there,
rolling with the hills
in aesthetic commerce
is the tree.

The tree in our head
is a perfect tree;
a eulogised tree
an apostrophised tree
a tree of tarnished copper plaques;
Oh eucharistical tree,
you are now a patch of weeds
which the cows leave alone,
and yet once
you were
the largest emporium, the store
which sold everything,
in the Southern hemisphere:

After the 1901 fire
the Anthony Hordern building re-building
used 365 miles of hardwood and Kauri pine,
10,000,000 bricks
50,000 bags of cement
8,000 sheets of corrugated iron
1 acre of window glass.

Hosiery, pith helmet and glove
departments, three Anthonys
one William and many

Johns to marry, carry and let
society talk about. The weight
of being famous; of branches
propped up with pylons;
behind countless counters,
pythons charming customers
with the latest Tanganyikan
tapioca tribal atrocity.

The weight of representing
so many things at once.

when I die we'll rot

They came from Spain
into Africa and drove to Picton
to drill holes and pour poison
through the king's ear. You cannot stop
the vandals. They came
to usurp the aweful power
of a tree.

The tree
lost its hold
and in the long span
of things, tens of years,
grew poor beside its sign;
and the company grew
gaunt and failed to paint
its stature on the hills
one year; and so the sign
flaked. Then one day

a Hordern boy looked
at the tree and felt the poison in his stems
and branches turning firewood
and his foundations faltered
when he saw the congruence
of Company and Tree.

what do you do when a metaphor changes your mind?

You look blank. Your face
is wiped by the suggestion.
There is no tree, there has been
no tree. You look in my face
for quaintness, and I reply: "Take
the F5 to Goulburn and look
for the sign 'Johnson & Johnson' –
behind that sign you shall find
a tree."

Now, to go back to the classic dieback situation, which
we had in the beginning, as long
ago as 1864. Again, it was observed in the 1880's, and
an agricultural officer was sent to Glen Innes to have a look;
and he didn't come up with very much, except to say
that thousands of hectares of trees had died.
So this dieback has been going on for a long
long time … but then you get human intervention. The squatters
went out into the Western districts and the Tableland
areas and started clearing paddocks to graze in.

They isolated trees.
Continuous forest or woodland ended up ... a tree here ...
a bunch of trees there, for cattle to shade under; and that's
where the trouble began to loom, the balance of recovery
went against the tree.

season to taste

We are building on the emotion of sparseness,
we are playing with the natural humour
of the land and we are forcing the seasons
into our states of mind.

SPRING

In the 1950's, the major development of agriculture at that time,
was the introduction of aerial supering and a lot of land
which was hitherto unprofitable to manage, except
for rough grazing, suddenly became quite worthwhile.

I understand, we have completely demolished the phosphate islands in the Pacific
to feed our supply.

squeeze me

Come,
come into this jungle and be

maudlin – be soft amongst these spikes –
let us press them in, let us blubber
and wail, let those trees draw it out
of us till we swell up – great fleshy
succulents, melodramatic toads; come
come, feel what it is to be ninety
percent water – get your hands around your
waste and scream ...

Then
come, slip into the mangle
of the bush and wring, wring the fine
freelance; call until you can
no more. The bush, the ambush of fractions
and treasons says merge,
partake of parasites and epiphytes
and mutualists bent on advantageous flair –
let this be your lush time, your epidural
for endurance, take it in your spine and sink
stomach first into the cobweb twigs – Beauty
Sleeping, this is your chance
it's the closest thing you'll get
to Europe and Romance.

SUMMER

*The Christmas beetle starts out life as a grub, in the ground
they feed off roots and grasses. They live there for about
three to five years, according to their species, and under*

the right conditions in Summer, on a nice moist Summer day,
they pupate. They go into a pupal stage and emerge
as young adults to the surface of the pasture.
They immediately fly away in large swarms and they
only feed in semi-sunlight, they don't like shaded
areas, and will never graze the underside of a tree,
at least not initially.
If you get a very hot, dry drought type Summer, the surface
of the soil bakes; the pupative adult can't chew its way
to the surface and it dies.

There is no distance in the bush
only a game between twigs; this place
is a ruin of twigs, a revolt, a comedy.
Trees with mostly smooth, white
reddish or blue bark
without scribbles;
trees with mostly smooth, white
or blue bark usually with
scribbles;
trees with rough, stringy – fibrous
bark over some or all
of the trunk;
trees with rough, flaky
bark over most
of the trunk;
trees with very hard, rough
'iron bark';
trees with a short fibrous
'box' type of bark –
and all of them

with twigs.
Everything here has learnt to imitate
twigs; the birds
are short, brown twigs
with fat leaves; the insects
are shattered twigs; and the snakes
are pretending to be the
bastards which flick up
and grate your shin and jab
your calf with fat glossy fun,
shooting like a slapstick gun.

AUTUMN

There is also the leaf
beetle which has two life cycles each year. The eggs
are laid on the leaves so the larvae feed on the leaves
and then they pupate and grow into adults. The beetles stay
and feed on the leaves as well. So there you've got three
predators – and what has happened to the tree?
The tuber is responding to the loss
of leaves through the Christmas beetle –
so about this time, early Autumn, they put out a crop of leaves.
Along comes the second life cycle of the leaf eating beetle –
and chews it down. The tree continues to send starch
up to put out new leaves and in late Autumn we get a frost
and those immature leaves, before they have even
come out, are shrivelled up and they die.
And that's the sort of cycle
that's been happening.

pickles, relish and preserves

And the onus is on you, on you
the onus repeats, it's on you
it beats into you, the waiting, the maidens
moated. Dormant for a hundred years
or picking flowers, waiting to be broken, all of them
floating, stooping, all of them
low-slung, dangling – it must have hurt Rapunzel so –
the weight; Mariana, Maud and Proserpine
it is time to be taken to the underworld,
lie chastened against your master's roots, or thorns
or thick-moated sunbeam – your youth,
that writhing jealousy – don't look to the face,
the green has paled, dropped, your womanly virtue
is patience and your feature, say it – your hymen
is undone. Mother Earth, our trees don't drop all
their leaves, but our women, yes, they wait in forests
far more bright than that of pines or oaks – but
protected
they wait and they become the flesh,
they form tubers and pupate. Mellifluous women,
you are the fat silence of Nature. Feed and wait.
For the Eucalypt must have its tuber, and the scarab
must pupate, and you must palliate awkward,
unaesthetic things with the softness and the sweetness
of your fall.

what... no pudding?

WINTER

Now the real problem is, of course, that it's moved
from being simply a scientific one, to a social one. Very few
farmers are prepared to sacrifice a large area of their
properties to trees.
It impedes their agricultural production because
trees get in the way. The other problem is that for years and years
and years people have been ringbarking
trees and despite the fact that we've got widespread
dieback, the thing that amazed me when I drove
through Glen Innes last year in May, was that I actually saw
a person still
ringbarking to clear a corner of his property out.
There's no legislation to say a fellow can't do that,
but it seems to me that, when we're running out of trees,
that's the last thing anyone should be
encouraged to do.

And there are a number of other causes of dieback which, because of the Christmas
beetle one, have sort of been overlooked.

How many times
have I sat alone and cried.
I have been in a desolate place
with no future but a thick past, thick with things
gone strange, highly coloured then dead.
I am there now,
it has been the same, so heavy
and so many times; it is like a cycle –
I live through all the seasons

and increase the rings of memory
in my brain. My brain hardly notices
the repetition.

The Winter of singularities is upon us; yes
Summer had bachelor outlines too – but
here, it is not so much the trees that change,
the emotions swap, within a lump of so-called time.

Where is the tuber of my new
growth; where are the thick clotted leaves –
I am all undone – ransacked or burnt
or eaten.

I shall dry
from the outside
in; die by degrees from the tip
backwards; die because there is
no drought. Drought?
Plague.

We are on a Ferris wheel,
courtesy, through the –
compliment – may I have the,
pressure – and the centrifugal force
is tight and exciting,
spin with despair, it's a jubilee –
my mind, my slavish mind, should lose its, should lose,

will ease, release, leash, itch, list, gist –

catafalque, catafalque, my bier. Goodnight.

eno? Or a couple of alka seltzers

SPRING

The glare of the sun
in the grass
says plant more
plant again, try for the artifice
of smallness
that will grow.
Choose trees
that are hardy, unwanted
and unknown
and pretend
that the halo of effervescence
blesses them –
that the whirring fizz
is life; that what seems
to be the excitement of growth
is not
the eating
of glare harassed
beetles; that what
you have offered
will not

become less; that the
matches in this hand
are not
for fire; that your
despair
is not
to visit you
again; that you have land
which no longer cries, but accepts
its hard term
in history; that you have not found
failure
to be alive
and living off
your slightest
thought; pretend that you have gone
to hell
intact.

Repeat after me:
Eucalyptus nova-anglica,
E. blakelyi, E. stellulata and E.
calliginosa; forgive them
for they know not,
forgive them
what
they do.

envoi:

I had a tree which sang me songs

    I don't mind where you go
    I don't mind what you do
    Who you are – I don't care

I had a tree and sang it songs

    Grow for me, grow for me
    I care, I care
    I am hard by, hard by you

I had a tree

    I'll look after you, I said
    When I have the time
    After all, you're always there

I had a tree, its leaves hummed and curled

    What is this net
    This net cast over me?
    Your eyes have woven
    Such a mesh, a mesh which stands
    In place of me.